D1168797

I must conquer my loneliness

alone.

I must be happy with myself
or I have
nothing
to offer you.

Two halves have
little choice
but to
join;
and yes,
they do
make a
whole

but two
wholes
when they coincide…

that is
beauty

that is
love.

Catch Me with Your Smile

by Peter McWilliams

Cover design by Paul LeBus
Interior design by Victoria Marine

Published by
Prelude Press
8165 Mannix Drive
Los Angeles, California 90046
213-650-9571

Other books by Peter McWilliams:

POETRY

Come Love with Me and Be My Life
For Lovers and No Others
The Hard Stuff: Love
Love: An Experience Of
Love Is Yes
Come To My Senses
Catch Me with Your Smile
I Marry You Because...

PERSONAL GROWTH

How to Survive The Loss of a Love
(with Melba Colgrove, Ph.D.
and Harold Bloomfield, M.D.)

You Can't Afford the Luxury
of a Negative Thought
(with John-Roger)

COMPUTERS

The Personal Computer Book

Published by and available from

Prelude Press
8165 Mannix Drive
Los Angeles, California 90046
213-650-9571

Catch Me with Your Smile

There
you were
dancing.

I saw only your back first.
Then a hint of your profile.
But even then I knew
my search had found
in you a fulfillment.

The long search.

The search I would abandon,
and then realize that the search
included that abandonment.

There
you were,
dancing.

I am not
a total
stranger.

I am a
perfect
stranger.

"I feel an affinity for you.."

I guess that's as close
as clever people ever
come to saying
"I love you."

On the first date.

Am I mad?

Am I remarkably lonely
or remarkably perceptive?

How can I be feeling such caring
and tenderness and devotion?

How can I be feeling this
so soon? How have I lasted
without it so long?

It is a risk to love.

What if it doesn't
work out?

Ah,
but what if it does.

I want to
explore the delights
of
one-to-one
human emotion
with you.

I want to say
whatever words
need be said
to get words
out of the way.

I am impatient.
I am frightened.
I am fascinated.
I am in love with you.

I don't want
to build my
life around
you,

but I want to
include you
in the building
of my life.

All I know is that

I love you.
I want you.
Some times I need you.

You are someone
and being with you something
I
long for.

And I love you.

That's all I know

Missing you

could turn from

pain
to
pleasure

if only I knew

you

were missing me

too.

This whole lifetime spent
growing and learning and
risking and failing and
succeeding and selecting
and gathering and prepairing.

I had begun to wonder:
What is all this for?

And now comes the answer.

You.

Every time I do
something wonderful
I immediately think
of sharing it with you.

The longing
The laughing
The loving
The living

The joy
The pain
The sun
The rain

Thank you.

I am in love again.

Everyone sighs at
sunsets and roses.

I sigh at
sunsets and roses
and you.

Airports. Cabs. Hotels.
Airports. Rent-a-cars.
Airports.

The world is not very real.

Sometimes only the memory
of you keeps me going.

I await the reality of
your embrace.

In those rare
moments when
all desires
have been fulfilled,

my mind
rests
on only
you.

This,
for me,
is love.

I know
love
because
I know
you.

I know
you
because
I know
love.

If
I give you
a reason
for loving,

You give
me
a reason
for living.

The world is good.

I feel whole & directed.

Touch my Joy with me.

I cannot keep
my smiles
in single file.

I sit
atop
the
Empire State
thinking
thoughts
of my
love
for
you.

And the
TV transmitter
above me,
with all its
millions and
billions of
kilowatts,
cannot
impress the
Universe
one million-billionth
as much
as the
love-thoughts
I
send
to
you.

What a wonderful
place this is,
loving you.

Writing
a poem
of our
love

is
like

coloring
a
color.

I cannot write of
my love for you.

I cannot select the proper
words and phrases.

I have lost my discrimination.

Since you,
everything is good.

You
are the nicest
thing I could
ever do for
myself.

I don't know whether
I want you because I love you
or
I love you because I want you.

Which came first,
the chicken
or Colonel Sanders?

I do know that I
love being with you and
I like thinking about you.

My love is with you this day.

Perfect joy and
perfect sorrow.

One following another
following another.

The poles, the extremes,
of emotional life and
all points in between.

Following one another.
Following one another.

Gently up, gently down
like the ocean under a boat.

Your Joy
is my
desire.

Your happiness
my vocation.

your fulfillment
my goal.

If you
love me,
tell me
so.

If you
tell me
love me
so.

You have
great power
over my love.

My love has
great power
over me.

I am young
so love is new.

There is so much
I want to know
about you.

So many things I
want to do
with you.

So many
embraces.

So many
moments.

I have
nothing
to share
with you
but my
life.

I have
nothing
to experience
with you
but our
love.

This is all.

Is all enough?

Joy
is a word I use
to describe our
love.

Love
is a word I use
to describe our
joy.

I am
in love
with you

that is

I am in love,

hoping you'll
join me.

Even on the
busiest of days,
I think about you
every other thought.

Ecstasy.

say the
word aloud:

ecstasy.

shout the
word, as
loud as
you
are able:

ECSTASY!

softly,
gently,
tenderly,
breathe
the word:

ecstasy.

and
this
is
my
love.

We've both been kicking
around the universe for
some time now, alone,
and doing all right.

But somewhere in the
back of our hearts
was a tugging
—not a perpetual longing,
but some subtle gnawing—
that we might be better
together than
alone apart;
not too dependent,
not too independent,
but rather like the
baby bear's porridge:
Just Right.

I enjoy you.

your body.
your life style.
your appreciation of me.
your warmth.
your hesitancy to speak &
your freedom to touch.

In holding you I am held.

This poem
is a kiss
for your mind.

Life is
not a
struggle.

It's a
wiggle.

If the purpose of life is loving,
the purpose of my life is loving
you.

The difference between
love and loving

is the difference between
fish and fishing.

Does the earth
have a sky
or
does the sky
have an earth?

Does the body
have an aura
or
does the aura
have a body?

Do we have love
or
does love have us?

I've heard a lot
about the dangers of
living beyond one's means.

What worries me, however,
is my current habit of
living beyond my meanings.

The world outside
is a mirror,
reflecting the

good & bad
joy & sorrow
laughter & tears

within me.

Some people are
difficult mirrors
to look into,

but you…

I look at you
and I see
all the beauty
inside of me.

Row
row
row
romance,

gently down the
stream, merrily,
merrily, merrily,
marry me. life
is but a dream.

Why do I
think of
Christmas
when I see
a rose?

Is it the
red and the green
or is it the
love?

My love is
not
a red red rose;

for red red roses
with today's advanced
methods of cross-
pollination are much
too common.

Find me a flower
that is
beguiling,
whimsical,
lyrical,
many-faceted,
perfectly imperfect,
and
one of a kind.

Give it a
name that
matches its
uniqueness

and to this
I may dare
to compare
My love.

You are now
a part of my life.

In all decisions
you are a consideration.

In all problems
(mostly in terms
of solution)
you
are a factor.

In all Joy you are
sharing, in all sorrow
support.

I love you my friend.

I am a friend to you
my love.

My love and
God's Light
be with you

in all that
you are and
in all that
you do.

I am
falling faster
than I said
I would
or thought
I could…

And you aren't
helping any.

You're so
comforting
&
creative
&
beautiful
&
full filling…

I am falling
I will flap my arms
and pretend to be flying.

Help me.
Break my
fall.
Catch me
with your smile.